WORKING ANIMALS

Police

WORKING ANIMALS
Police

Jim Mezzanotte

Marshall Cavendish
Benchmark
New York

Library of Congress Cataloging-in-Publication Data

Mezzanotte, Jim.
  Police / Jim Mezzanotte.
     p. cm. – (Working animals)
  Includes index.
  Summary: "Describes animals, such as dogs and horses, which work with police in such areas as search-and-rescue, tracking criminals, and sniffing out explosives"–Provided by publisher.
  ISBN 978-1-60870-166-7
  1. Animals in police work–Juvenile literature. 2. Police dogs–Juvenile literature. 3. Police horses–Juvenile literature. 4. Vocational guidance–Juvenile literature. I. Title.
  HV8025.M49 2010
  363.2–dc22
                                        2010007006

Editorial and design by
Amber Books Ltd
Bradley's Close
74–77 White Lion Street
London N1 9PF
United Kingdom
www.amberbooks.co.uk

Project Editor: James Bennett
Copy Editor: Peter Mavrikis
Design: Andrew Easton
Picture Research: Terry Forshaw, Natascha Spargo

Printed in China
135642

CONTENTS

Chapter 1
Helping Police

Do you like animals? Maybe you have a pet dog or cat, or even a horse. These animals can become lifelong companions. But they can be more than just pets. They can work at important jobs helping police around the world.

Police Dogs

Dogs have been helping police for hundreds of years. In the late 1800s, police in Ghent, Belgium, began taking dogs along as they patrolled the city streets. By the early 1900s, many other cities around the world were also using dogs to help fight crime.

Today most big cities have dogs on the police force. Each dog gets paired with a police officer, called a handler. Together they make up a **K-9 unit**. ("K-9" sounds like "canine," which is another word for a dog.)

◄ **A bloodhound leads his handler on a search for an escaped prisoner.**

▲ **A yellow Labrador retriever searches an airport for illegal drugs.**

《Many police departments use German shepherds for K-9 units, but some also use Belgian Malinois or Doberman pinschers.》

K-9 dogs help fight crime in many ways. On patrol with officers, they help catch criminals. They also help keep crowds under control during public gatherings, such as rallies or protests. Dogs have a very good sense of smell, so police dogs use their noses, too. They sniff out criminals hiding in buildings. Or their noses lead them to illegal drugs or evidence of a crime.

Police use dogs for other jobs, too. Dogs can sniff out and find bombs. They can **track** criminals who are trying to escape. They can also find people who are missing, and rescue them if they are in trouble.

The kind of dog the police use usually depends on the job. Many police departments use German shepherds for K-9 units, but some also use Belgian Malinois or Doberman pinschers. Police may use Labrador retrievers for finding things such as drugs or bombs. Bloodhounds are good at tracking people, while Newfoundlands and Saint Bernards are often used for rescues.

◄ **These dogs are training to help police control crowds of people.**

Search and Rescue on 9/11

On September 11, 2001, terrorists hijacked planes and flew them into the World Trade Center towers, in New York City, and the Pentagon building, in Washington, D.C. A short time later, both towers in New York collapsed.

Search-and-rescue teams quickly responded. They came from all over the country, and other countries, too. Professional emergency workers—including police officers, firefighters, and medical personnel—and volunteers worked day and night searching for people buried in the wreckage. Dogs were a big part of the effort. Their strong sense of smell helped them find victims that humans could not detect. The work was tough and also dangerous. The dogs had to climb through tangles of sharp steel and glass. They had to avoid falling into deep holes and areas that were still dangerously hot. They were also breathing in toxic dust and fumes. But the dogs kept searching, often working twelve-hour shifts.

Sirius, a bomb-sniffing dog, was killed in the attack. When the planes hit the World Trade Center, Sirius and his handler were at a police station in one of the towers. The handler left Sirius to go help others. Before he could return, the tower collapsed. Months later, Sirius was found in the wreckage. A memorial service was later held for Sirius, and the dog was given full police honors, including a twenty-one gun salute.

▲ **A picture of Sirius was displayed during the dog's memorial service.**

“By the late 1800s, many big cities in the United States had mounted police units that rode horses.”

Police Horses

For centuries, horses have been helping people—including the police. Long before cars were invented, sheriffs and deputies got around on horseback, easily traveling long distances. Horses were useful in big cities, too. As far back as the 1700s, police in London patrolled the city on horseback. By the late 1800s, many big cities in the

▼ In the 1800s, this horse helped police patrol the streets of London. The earliest mounted police officers were recruited from the cavalry.

Dogs, Horses, and People

Dogs and horses have helped people for a very long time. Scientists believe that dogs were **domesticated** more than 14,000 years ago and that their ancestors were wolves. At first, dogs might have just stayed close to people in order to **scavenge** for food. Eventually, dogs and people felt comfortable enough around each other that they began living together. The dogs could help protect a settlement, and they could even help move loads by pulling sleds. After a while, certain kinds of dogs did specific jobs. Some dogs helped with hunting, by tracking and attacking prey. Other dogs helped herd animals, such as sheep.

People hunted horses long before they domesticated them. About 40,000 years ago, people were hunting wild horses that roamed grassy plains in Europe and Asia. Then, about 5,000 years ago, people domesticated horses. At first, they only used the horses for meat and milk. A few thousand years later, people had other sources of food. They soon learned to ride horses and used them to pull carts. Since then, horses have had a huge impact on human history. With horses, people were able to travel great distances and pull heavy loads. Horses also helped armies win wars. For thousands of years, until trains and cars came along, a horse was the main way of getting around quickly on land.

▲ **This police dog patrolled the streets of New York City at the turn of the twentieth century.**

" The U.S. Border Patrol uses horses to guard remote areas along the Mexican border. Police sometimes ride horses during search-and-rescue missions, too. "

United States had **mounted police** units that rode horses.

In the twentieth century, cars came along, and most police departments stopped using horses. Today, however, big cities in many different countries still have mounted police units. Like a K-9 unit, horse and rider work together. They patrol the city,

making sure there is no criminal activity. Or they help control large crowds during public events. In parks and other rural areas, police ride horses where it's hard for cars or trucks to travel. The U.S. Border Patrol uses horses to guard remote areas along the Mexican border. Police sometimes ride horses during search-and-rescue missions, too.

Different breeds of horses are used for police work. Most police departments use horses that are donated to them. The horses are often older, and they may have done other kinds of jobs earlier in life, such as working on ranches or in rodeos. In the United States, the most popular breed of horse used by police departments is the **quarter horse**. Police also use **draft horses**, such as Percherons, as well as Tennessee walking horses. They also use horses

◄ **These police horses are on duty in Dublin, Ireland.**

that are different breeds mixed together. Even thoroughbred racing horses have had second careers working for the police.

Everyday Heroes

Horses and dogs in law enforcement do a great service for their communities, saving lives and helping people in many different ways. Sometimes, they are hurt or even killed in the line of duty. Police dogs, for example, may get shot by criminals. Horses may stumble on bumpy streets or get struck by vehicles. Sometimes, people even throw things at them.

These animals are part of the force, just like police officers. Police departments make sure the animals stay healthy and get a lot of care and attention. When the animals retire from police work, police departments make sure they go to good homes.

▲ A K-9 team rides the subway in New York with other passengers.

Chapter 2
K-9 Patrol

In a K-9 unit, the dog and handler are partners who depend on each other. Unlike most police units, a K-9 team stays together twenty-four hours a day. The dog and handler live together, and the dog becomes part of the handler's family.

Out on Patrol

K-9 units usually go out on patrol on a daily basis. They help keep the peace, and they catch criminals. They often patrol in the afternoon and at night, when the most trouble happens. The dog and handler ride together in a special car or sport utility vehicle (SUV) that is set up to transport the dog.

The unit may get a call that a robbery has taken place. The K-9 unit arrives at the scene. Criminals may be hiding inside a building. The

◀ **This New York City K-9 unit is standing guard on New Year's Eve.**

▲ **People must wear thick padding when they train police dogs!**

❝Most criminals are afraid of police dogs, and they usually surrender. But dogs can also chase criminals who try to escape.❞

handler lets the dog go in to investigate first. If the dog's sharp sense of smell detects the criminals, he will notify his handler by barking. Most criminals are afraid of police dogs, and they usually surrender. But dogs can also chase criminals who try to escape. Many dogs are trained to "bite and hold." They clamp onto the suspect's arm and hold until the officer can put on the handcuffs. Big dogs have strong jaws—some of

▲ **Police officers in Chengdu, China, train German shepherds to chase suspected criminals.**

Obedience Training

Before dogs are trained for police work, they receive basic obedience training. They learn to obey basic commands from their handlers, such as "sit," "stay," "come," and "heel" (walk by the handler's side). All police dogs get obedience training.

This training is based on conditioning, just like training for police work. The handler conditions a dog to do something, such as sit. Each time the dog sits, the dog gets a reward, such as a treat or a toy. The reward is called a reinforcer. Handlers never use physical violence when training dogs.

Many dog trainers also use clicker training. A clicker helps a dog learn which action to repeat to get a reward. A dog may sit, for example, but then roll over. The handler doesn't give the reward then, because the dog will think it's for rolling over. So, the handler uses a clicker at the exact moment the dog sits. The dog hears the clicking sound and knows the reward is coming. The dog also knows the reward is for sitting, and not for rolling over. After a while, the handler uses a command instead of a clicking sound.

Obedience training is very important for dogs. It helps dogs develop a strong bond with the people who train them, based on trust and mutual respect.

▲ **Police dogs always respond to a handler's command—such as to "heel," or walk by the handler's side.**

"Getting a tip on a drug dealer, the team may go to the suspect's house, where the dog sniffs out and finds drugs."

them can clamp down with a force of 300 pounds (91 kilograms)! Some police dogs "bark and hold." They keep watch over a suspect without biting, and they bark if the suspect tries to escape.

The K-9 unit may do other jobs, too. Getting a tip on a drug dealer, the team may go to the suspect's house, where the dog sniffs out and finds drugs. Or the unit may go to a crime scene, so the dog can sniff for evidence. If there is a public rally or protest, the K-9 unit will make sure there is no violence or other problems. Sometimes just the sight of a police dog makes people less likely to cause trouble.

Although most police dogs do a variety of jobs, some are trained for special tasks. They may be experts at tracking criminals who have escaped

and are on the run. Or they might be skilled in sniffing out bombs, either in buildings or at airports. Unlike other police dogs, bomb-sniffing dogs do not retrieve what they find. If they did, the bomb might explode! Instead, they sit calmly and wait for their handlers.

Dog Welfare

Police dogs have dangerous jobs. They must often deal with violent criminals. Some dogs even wear bulletproof vests for protection. Police dogs always try to protect their handlers, even if that means risking their own lives. In some cases, police departments have erected monuments to dogs that were killed in the line of duty. In Miami, Florida, for example, a memorial honors the city's slain

▶ **This police dog is a Belgian Malinois, a kind of dog often used for police work.**

Born to Help

German shepherds and Belgian Malinois make good police dogs. But long before they were helping the police, they were helping farmers. These dogs are herding dogs. They were first used by farmers to herd and protect sheep.

A German military officer started the German shepherd breed in the late 1800s. He wanted to create the ideal working dog—smart, loyal, and strong. During World War I, the dogs helped the German army. Soldiers from other countries were impressed with the breed. One American soldier found a German shepherd puppy during the war. He named the dog Rin Tin Tin. The soldier took the dog back to the United States, and Rin Tin Tin soon became a star in the movies. Besides helping police with patrols and search and rescue, German shepherds also work as guide

dogs. They help visually impaired people to get around.

Belgian Malinois get their name from the Belgian city of Mechelen (Malines in French), where the breed was first developed. The dogs look similar to German shepherds, but they are smaller and lighter in weight. These high-energy dogs also tend to be quicker and more agile than German shepherds. The United States Secret Service, which protects the president and other government figures, uses Belgian Malinois to search for explosives.

▲ **In the 1950s, many Americans watched a TV show called the *The Adventures of Rin Tin Tin*, which starred a German shepherd.**

" Most police dogs work about five or six years and then retire. They usually stay with the handler. In some cases, the handler retires, too!"

police dogs. In Salt Lake City, Utah, a memorial for Utah police officers includes a bronze sculpture of a K-9 officer and her dog.

Police handlers must care for their partners every single day. They make sure the dogs are properly fed and bathed and get regular checkups by a **veterinarian**. Most police dogs work about five or six years and then retire. They usually stay with the handler. In some cases, the handler retires, too!

Dog Training

Not many dogs have what it takes to be in a K-9 unit. Police dogs must be strong and **agile**, but they can't be too active or excitable. They must stay calm, even around loud noises and a lot of action. Police dogs must be brave and **aggressive**, but they

must also get along well with people.

German shepherds have all these qualities, which is why police departments often use them. They are big, smart dogs that learn quickly.

▶ **German shepherds are smart and alert, and make excellent police dogs.**

▲ People at a fair got to watch this police dog in action during a K-9 demonstration in Gainesville, Florida.

« All police dogs, no matter how different, have one thing in common. They have gone through extensive training to do their jobs. »

They are also friendly to people and very loyal to their handlers. Other breeds also make good police dogs, depending on the job they will do. All police dogs, no matter how different, have one thing in common. They have gone through extensive training to do their jobs.

Police departments find and train their dogs in many different ways. Some departments use dogs that are donated to them. The dog handlers

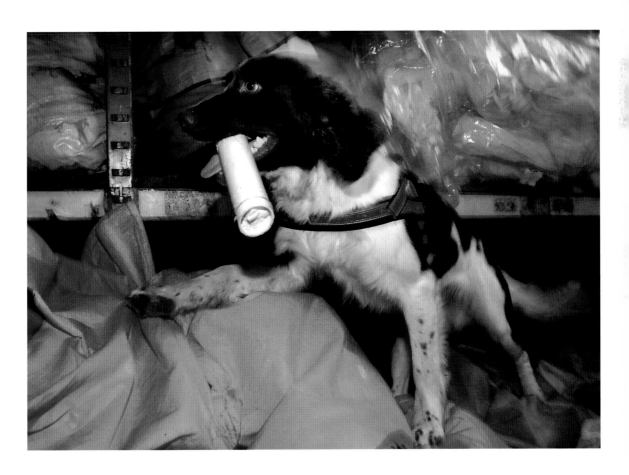

▲ **This Springer Spaniel is searching for drugs in a prison.**

"Handlers use rewards to train the dogs. When the dogs do something correctly, the handlers praise them and give them a treat."

then train the dogs themselves. Other police departments buy dogs that have already been specially trained for police work. They usually get these dogs from European countries, such as Germany or the Netherlands. When the dogs arrive, the handlers go through training to learn how to communicate and work with the animals. Most police dogs are male. They usually start training when they are adults, at about two years of age.

Police dogs get a lot of training. They learn to obey commands from their handlers. They go through obstacle courses, crawling out of windows and through tunnels, climbing up ladders and over walls. Guns are fired near them, so they get used to the loud noise. Handlers use rewards to train the dogs. When the dogs do something correctly, the handlers praise them and give them a treat.

For the dogs, training often means playing games. To train a dog to sniff out drugs, for example, the handler might use a rolled-up towel for playing tug-of-war. This towel becomes the dog's new toy. After a while, the handler puts some drugs in the towel. The handler then hides the towel and the dog has to find it. For the dog, the smell of drugs means the toy is nearby. When he sniffs for drugs, he's actually looking for his toy!

Training a dog to "bite and hold" works much the same way. A trainer wears thick padding on one arm. Another trainer commands the dog to clamp onto the padded arm. Then the dog gets praise and a treat. He's not a mean dog attacking—instead, he's playing a kind of game, with a reward at the end.

Dog training usually takes several weeks. But the training doesn't end then. Police dogs keep getting trained throughout their careers.

▶ **Police dogs ride in vehicles that are specially equipped to carry them.**

Raising Money for Police Dogs

For police dogs, staying safe isn't a simple task—especially when they don't have all the protection they need. Each year, police dogs are killed or injured by gunfire. Bulletproof vests help protect the dogs when criminals start shooting. But the vests are expensive, and many police departments cannot afford to buy them.

In several states, children have come to the rescue. In Florida, a girl named Stacey Hillman decided to raise money so dogs in her state could have bulletproof vests. She started by putting collection jars in veterinarian offices and pet stores. Eventually, she raised more than $100,000. In California, a girl named Alyssa Mayorga read about a police dog that had been killed in action. She'd been saving pennies she found on the street. After reading this story, she decided she would give the money to the police department to buy bulletproof vests. People in other states have also raised money to buy vests for police dogs.

▲ **This police dog, named Kazan, is wearing a new bulletproof vest that will help him to stay safe.**

"Bulletproof vests help protect dogs when criminals start shooting. But the vests are expensive, and many police departments cannot afford to buy them."

Standing Trial

Sometimes a police department must go to court to defend itself against a person it has caught committing a crime. The person has filed a lawsuit saying that the dog used too much force and hurt the person. But when the police prove that the dog had been given proper training, they usually win the case.

▲ **A well-trained police dog is not mean or vicious. The dog is just doing his job!**

Beagle Brigade

Beagles are small dogs. They don't get used often for police work. But some beagles do a special job for the U.S. government. This team of dogs is called the Beagle Brigade. They work at airports, where they sniff out agricultural products, such as fruits and meats. When people return from other countries, they are not allowed to bring back these products. The products may carry pests and diseases, which cause big problems for farmers in the United States. But, some people may try to sneak in the products in their luggage.

The beagles help with this problem. They work well in crowded airports, where some people might be intimidated by larger dogs. Beagles also have an excellent sense of smell. They can also tell apart many different kinds of smells. This ability allows a beagle to smell a certain type of food that should not be in a person's luggage. Once this food is discovered, the beagle sits next to the luggage, so the dog's handler knows to check it.

▲ **A member of the Beagle Brigade sniffs some luggage at JFK Airport in New York City.**

Sniffing for Phones

In the United States, police are training dogs to sniff out something unusual—cell phones! The dogs work in prisons, where cell phones are a big problem. Prisoners are not allowed to have cell phones, but the phones often get smuggled inside. They are also easy to hide. Prisoners often use the phones to carry out more crimes. Although they're behind bars, they can plan crimes with other criminals who are not in prison. They may plan escapes, or they may threaten victims who are scheduled to testify against them in court. Prison officials could block the phone signals, so prisoners could not make calls. But if they did, they would block signals for other people in the area.

Police dogs solve the problem. Cell phones give off a particular scent, and the dogs have been specially trained to recognize it. When they arrive at a prison, they locate the phones quickly. They have found phones in all kinds of places—hidden inside books, as well as inside shoes, brushes, lights, and even food! Police officials have mostly been using German shepherds, Belgian Malinois, and Labradors to do this important work.

▲ **Police dogs can be trained to sniff out many things, including cell phones.**

Chapter 3
Mounted Police

Like a K-9 unit, the horse and rider in a mounted police unit are a team. They spend many hours a day together. The officer takes good care of the horse, and the horse has complete trust in the officer. They develop a strong bond.

City Patrol

Most mounted police units are found in cities. London, for example, has more than one hundred horses in its mounted police unit. In the United States, New York City and San Francisco have two of the nation's oldest mounted police units, and many other cities have mounted police as well.

Mounted police usually go out on patrols, just like K-9 units. They patrol parks and neighborhoods, helping to keep the peace and fight crime.

◄ **In Russia, mounted police watch for trouble as fans buy tickets to a soccer match.**

▲ **In Los Angeles, mounted police officers take part in a parade.**

❝Mounted police may help direct traffic. They can also chase suspects into areas where squad cars can't go.❞

Police officers on horses are about 10 feet (3 meters) off the ground. When they patrol, they can often spot trouble more easily than officers on foot or in cars. Being so high up, they are also visible to others, so people know the police are around.

Mounted police may help direct traffic. They can also chase suspects into areas where squad cars can't go.

Controlling Crowds

Another important job for mounted police is helping to control large

▲ **A police officer watches a crowd of people as they celebrate after a baseball game. His job is easier because he is so high off the ground.**

Quick Quarter Horses

In the United States, many police departments use quarter horses for their mounted units. These horses are most often used by police in the western part of the country.

In the 1800s, quarter horses were a big help to cattle ranchers in the Southwest. The horses had "cow sense"—they were good at herding cattle. Cowboys rode quarter horses on cattle drives. They traveled long distances to bring the cattle to market. After a cattle drive, cowboys often held contests to see who had the best skills, such as riding a horse or roping cattle. From these contests, the modern rodeo was born. Today, ranchers still use quarter horses to herd cattle, and you can still find them performing in rodeos. Along with their riders, they compete in many events, such as barrel racing. In this event, horse and rider race around barrels, making very tight turns.

Quarter horses are powerful and fast. They get their name from racing. They are often used in short sprints that are a quarter of a mile (400 meters) in length. They run at top speed from start to finish. The fastest quarter horse has been clocked at more than 50 miles (80 kilometers) per hour!

▲ **Strong and fast, the quarter horse is a good fit for police work.**

« Mounted police can be especially good at handling large crowds. For many people, horses are not as threatening as police dogs. »

crowds of people. Mounted police often get sent to public gatherings, such as parades, concerts, sporting events, and rallies. They get sent to protests, too. They help make sure these gatherings are peaceful.

Mounted police can be especially good at handling large crowds. For many people, horses are not as threatening as police dogs. But a big horse is still **intimidating**. When mounted police walk through a crowd, most people get out of the way!

Making Friends

There is one more important job that mounted police often do. They get to know people! When people see an officer on a horse, they often walk up for a closer look. "People won't pet a police car," explains one horse trainer. "But they will definitely pet a horse."

Sometimes people who never talk to the police will wind up talking to an officer on a horse. Mounted police help build trust in communities, and they learn what goes on in them. They often ride in parades and even give riding demonstrations from time to time.

Gearing Up for the Job

Mounted police use a lot of harness equipment. This equipment is referred to as "tack" and includes the saddle and bridle. The bridle is used by a rider to control a horse. It consists of a set of straps that fit around a horse's head and hold a bit in the mount's mouth. The reins are attached to each side of the bit. When a rider pulls one of the reins, the horse moves in that direction. Horses in mounted police units often

▶ **Horses make it easy for police officers to make friends. This horse and rider are patrolling in London.**

Horse Care

Taking care of horses is hard work! Horses need a lot of care and attention. You must clean out their stalls, making sure they have a clean bedding of straw or wood shavings. You must make sure they have plenty to eat, too. Horses eat about half a bale of hay each day. The hay is usually a mix of grass and **alfalfa**. Horses also eat smaller amounts of grain. In addition, a horse will need a large container of clean water and a salt block that it can lick.

Grooming is a big part of horse care. You must groom the horse's mane, tail, and coat. To groom a horse, you usually start by rubbing its coat with a curry brush. This hard rubber brush loosens dirt that has settled below the surface. Then you must use other brushes to take away the dirt and smooth the horse's coat. Finally, you must also comb out the horse's mane and tail.

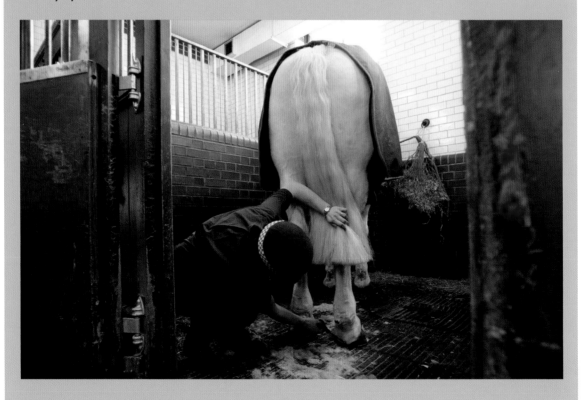

▲ **This police officer is grooming a horse in a police department stable. Horse care is an important part of a mounted officer's job.**

"The bridle is used by a rider to control a horse. It consists of a set of straps that fit around a horse's head and hold a bit in the mount's mouth."

wear special horseshoes on their hooves. These horseshoes help the horse walk on the hard concrete pavement common in cities. The horses may also wear saddlebags to hold the officer's equipment.

Officers also wear equipment. They carry guns and **batons**, and they may wear helmets, too. They also wear special pants and boots. The boots protect their legs in case the horse rubs against objects such

▲ **Police horses wear a lot of equipment. This horse is getting a special visor for protection, before it begins work controlling crowds during a soccer match.**

▲ Police horses can be any color. Here, two Russian mounted officers are riding white horses.

A Musical Ride

The Royal Canadian Mounted Police (RCMP) has been around since the 1800s. "Mounties" became famous for fighting crime on horseback. Today, however, they no longer use horses for police work. But officers in the RCMP still ride horses in the "Musical Ride." It is a performance put on by more than thirty horses and riders. They move together in complicated patterns that are set to music.

The Musical Ride began when Mounties still rode horses. It was a way for officers to show off their riding skills. The first official Musical Ride was held in 1887. By 1901, it had become a public event. Today police officers volunteer for the Musical Ride. They must go through months of intensive training. The officers may only stay for three years, so other officers get the chance to perform. They travel across Canada and to other parts of the world giving performances.

▲ As a crowd watches, members of the Royal Canadian Mounted Police perform a Musical Ride in Ottawa, the capital of Canada.

«Before working in a mounted police unit, horses get special training. This training helps prepare them for what they will face on the job.»

as the side of a building, a fence, or a tree.

Horse Training

Police departments have different ways of selecting and training their horses, just as they do with K-9 units. In many police departments, the horses are donated. The police may do their own training, or they may get outside help from professionals.

Very few horses are capable of working in a mounted police unit. The horses must be big, strong, and healthy. They must be able to follow orders, so they can't be stubborn. They can't be easily frightened, either, especially by crowds of people or loud noises. And they have to be quick learners who can get the job done.

Horses of all ages work in mounted police units, but police usually don't like using young, inexperienced mounts —they prefer horses that are at least six years old. The best police horses are often ones that have already done another kind of work. "Pick-up" horses are one example. They work at rodeos, picking up cowboys who have been thrown from bulls or bucking broncos. These horses don't mind working around noise and crowds. Ranch horses also make good police horses.

Before working in a mounted police unit, horses get special training. This training helps prepare them for what they will face on the job. They learn to trust the rider, even in frightening situations. Trainers ride the horses through water and other obstacles.

▶ **As part of their training for police work in the Czech Republic, these horses must learn to walk through thick smoke.**

Basic Training

Horses receive special training for police work. But, like dogs, they also get a lot of training early in their lives. The first stage of training begins in the first few days or weeks after horses are born. Trainers handle the **foals** and speak to them, so the foals get used to a human touch and voice. This early training teaches the young horses not to be afraid of people.

Many horses are not ridden until they are two or three years old. But, they still get a lot of training before then. When horses are **yearlings**, they get used to wearing a halter. They can be led around, and they will stop if commanded. They also learn to be calm when being groomed or checked by a veterinarian. Trainers may also place blankets on the horse's back, to get the horse ready to carry a saddle. When the horses get a little older, they begin ground training.

They get used to a saddle and bridle, and they get used to moving around in a small area, as the trainer tells them to start, stop, or change direction. Finally, trainers begin riding the horses. When horses have been properly trained beforehand, they usually don't mind being ridden.

▶ **A horse's basic training includes getting used to wearing a halter.**

They bring vehicles up close to the horse, including from behind, where the horse can't see. They make loud noises, using horns and even gunshots, and wave brightly colored flags. The horses may ride close to fire. They learn to accept people touching them.

Horse Welfare

In a mounted police unit, taking care of the horse is a big part of an officer's job. It's a way for the officers to build strong bonds with their horses. Officers make sure the horses get enough food and water. Horses should eat many small meals throughout the day, so the horses take a lot of breaks. The breaks also give the horses a rest. Officers groom their horses, too, so their coats stay shiny and clean. They also make sure the horses get regular medical checkups by a veterinarian.

▲ **A mounted police officer is just one of many officers taking part in this training exercise in San Diego, California. They are learning how to handle a riot.**

Finding Good Homes

Sometimes, police departments have to cut back or eliminate mounted units in order to save money. Other times, older horses need to retire. Fortunately, people often help to make sure the horses find good homes.

In 2009, for example, the police department in Tulsa, Oklahoma, got rid of its mounted unit. Eight horses needed new homes. A medical center in the area bought all the horses, so they could be used for community programs. The mounted police unit in Boston, Massachusetts, was first formed over one hundred years ago. In 2008, however, the city eliminated the unit and got rid of the horses. But five horses didn't travel far—they went to a county farm south of the city. The horses appear in parades and give rides to children. They also help the county's mounted unit with crowd control and search-and-rescue missions.

In the United Kingdom, the Horse Trust cares for many retired working horses, including police horses. It was founded in 1886 and is the oldest horse charity in the world. The Horse Trust cares for more than one hundred horses, ponies, and donkeys. Besides police horses, it also has military horses and race horses. The animals at the Horse Trust stay there for the rest of their lives.

▲ **A retired police horse goes out for a walk with his former handler.**

"When a horse is ready to retire, the police try to find it a good home. People who own horse farms often volunteer to take care of the retired mounts."

If the weather is very bad, officers may decide to keep the horses in their stables, especially if the streets are icy.

Police departments understand that the horses do a lot to help the community. When a horse is ready to retire, the police try to find it a good home. People who own horse farms often volunteer to take care of the retired mounts.

▲ **Like all horses, police horses need a stable that shelters them from the weather.**

Chapter 4
Search and Rescue

Sometimes, people get into trouble. They get lost or injured in the wilderness. A disaster, such as an earthquake or flood, might strike. A person might be trapped inside a collapsed building. That's when search-and-rescue (SAR) teams get to work.

The members of these teams are usually volunteers. But not being paid doesn't affect their performance. As soon as they get the call, they are ready to go. Dogs and horses are often part of an SAR team. They can do jobs that people and even machines cannot.

A Life-Saving Nose

While dogs are often used to sniff out drugs or explosives, they are also great at finding and rescuing people.

◄ **This German shepherd is searching the rubble after the terrorist attacks of September 11, 2001.**

▲ **A bloodhound can follow a trail that is many hours or even days old.**

Did you know you give off a scent, or smell? Every person does. Each day, millions of dead cells fall from your body. The cells are very tiny, so they are invisible. But dogs can smell them!

Tracking with Bloodhounds

Bloodhounds are among the best dogs for finding people. These dogs have a strong sense of smell. They also have a special ability to distinguish the scents of different people. If someone is lost, the SAR team uses something that touched the person, such as a shirt. The team lets the bloodhound smell it. Then the bloodhound begins "tracking" the person by following the scent along the ground. As bloodhounds track, they might sniff out the scents of many other people, but they still follow the scent of the missing person.

A bloodhound is also used to track the scent of a person suspected of a crime. The bloodhound's work is so trusted that it can even be used as evidence in a court of law.

▲ A dog helps search for survivors after a landslide in Chongqing, China.

▶ These bloodhounds are about to start searching for people.

"Many different breeds are good for air tracking. Search-and-rescue teams often use German shepherds, Belgian Malinois, and golden retrievers."

Sniffing the Air

Sometimes bloodhounds can't do their jobs. The scent trail may be too old, or the SAR team might not have anything that belonged to the missing person. The area to be searched might be very large, too. Tracking with bloodhounds can take a long time, because someone must follow right behind the dog.

In these cases, SAR teams use "air-tracking" dogs. These dogs do not sniff along the ground. Instead, they sniff the air for any human scent. They cannot tell apart different human scents. But they can run free, covering large areas quickly, and they let SAR teams know if any humans have been around. The dogs are good at finding people trapped in collapsed buildings, because they smell any human scent that rises up into the air.

Many different breeds are good for air tracking. Search-and-rescue teams often use German shepherds, Belgian Malinois, and golden retrievers. In snowy mountains, Saint Bernards search for people buried under avalanches. They smell the scent that rises up from the snow, and they dig down to the victims, opening air passages so that the victims can breathe. Newfoundlands are often used to rescue people in the water.

Like police dogs, SAR dogs get a lot of training. They must be strong, smart, and obedient. They can't be too aggressive, and they must work well in teams.

Mounted Search and Rescue

Horses can also be a big help to SAR teams. The horses can take the teams where cars or trucks might get stuck, such as marshy or sandy areas, or thick woods that are far from any roads. Mounted SAR teams can also travel much faster than teams on foot, and they can carry more equipment, such as medical supplies.

Sometimes the teams use helicopters along with horses to rescue a person.

Saving Swimmers

For hundreds of years, Newfoundland dogs have rescued people struggling in the water, such as swimmers and shipwrecked sailors. The dogs were first used on Newfoundland, an island in the North Atlantic that is part of Canada. The island's fishermen often took the dogs along with them when they went fishing. The dogs could pull heavy things from the water, such as fishing nets—and even people! On the island, the dogs could also be hitched to carts. Then they could pull fish and other loads, such as lumber.

Newfoundlands are some of the biggest and strongest dogs in the world. Some males have grown to be more than 6 feet (1.8 meters) long! The dogs are excellent swimmers, and they're well suited to the water. They have thick coats that are water-resistant, and they even have webbed feet. Newfoundlands might be huge, but they are also gentle. They are known for being good with children.

▲ **A Newfoundland takes part in a training lesson, learning how to rescue a swimmer.**

Saving Lives in the Swiss Alps

The Swiss Alpine Rescue Service helps save lives in the Swiss Alps, a mountain range in Switzerland. It is made up of volunteers and has over one hundred dog teams. If people get trapped in an avalanche, dog teams fly in by helicopter. Then, the dogs search for the victims. The dogs must find them quickly—people do not have a good chance of surviving after about thirty minutes. The dogs are trained for several years. During the winter season, a dog team is on call twenty-four hours a day and must be ready to go in minutes. The rescue teams often use German shepherds, but they also use Labradors and Border collies.

Saint Bernard dogs became famous for helping people in the Swiss Alps. The

dogs get their name from the Saint Bernard Pass. The pass is a route through the mountains that people have been using for thousands of years. Centuries ago, monks built a shelter for people traveling through the pass. The monks began using large, strong dogs to rescue people who got caught in avalanches or snowstorms. Eventually, these dogs came to be called Saint Bernards.

▲ **A fully grown Saint Bernard can weigh up to 260 pounds (118 kilograms). Today, Saint Bernards are not often used for mountain rescue work.**

For example, after the SAR workers locate the injured person, they radio a helicopter pilot who is standing by. The pilot can then land in a nearby clearing. The horses who work in this kind of situation must be specially trained so that they are not frightened by the noise of the helicopter.

Dogs and horses can also work together as part of an SAR team. As the dogs track a person, the team follows along on horseback.

SAR teams often come in to help with big disasters. After the terrorist attacks on September 11, 2001, SAR dogs and handlers were called. In New York City, they searched for people in the wreckage of the Twin Towers. SAR teams also looked for people at the damaged Pentagon building, in Washington, D.C. After Hurricane Katrina struck New Orleans and the surrounding area in 2005, SAR teams were there to help.

▲ **A search-and-rescue team on horseback goes to work in Mississippi in the aftermath of Hurricane Katrina.**

Chapter 5
Career Guide

Would you like a career working with police dogs or horses? There are several jobs that you could do. You could become a K-9 handler or be part of a mounted police unit. But first you must be a qualified police officer.

Police departments have different requirements for becoming an officer. You will have to finish high school. Some departments require that you go to college, too. You must pass tests showing that you are in top physical and mental shape. New officers often go to a police academy for training, which usually lasts several months.

As a police officer, you will do many jobs. You may direct traffic, or respond to an accident, or stop a burglary. You must work well with people, and you must be good at making decisions. A person's life may depend on your judgment!

Police work can be dangerous and stressful. The police department is

◀ **Before you can become a police dog handler, you must prove you are a good police officer.**

▲ **Sometimes, police dogs just have fun! This bomb-sniffing dog is playing catch with its handler.**

"K-9 handlers and mounted officers usually go through special training, just like the dogs and horses. They must learn how to work well with their animals."

never "closed." So officers work in shifts, including shifts in the middle of the night.

There is no easy way to become a K-9 handler or join a mounted police unit. Instead, officers usually get chosen after working on the force for many years. Competition for these jobs is often strong. In many cities, there may even be a waiting list. Only the best officers get selected. They have proven that they possess the right skills and experience for the job. K-9 handlers and mounted officers usually go through special training, just like the dogs and horses. They must learn how to work well with their animals.

Search and Rescue

Although many SAR teams are made up of volunteers, some people who go on search-and-rescue missions are professionals. They may be firefighters, police officers, or **paramedics**. In the United States, the Federal Emergency Management

◀ **Police dogs get a lot of training, which prepares them for the tough situations they'll face on the job.**

Speaking the Language

Many officers receive special training in order to become K-9 handlers. They may actually go through training with the dog, so they learn together as a team. Officers must learn how to handle the dog in different situations, such as controlling crowds or confronting a suspect. The handler and dog learn how to communicate with each other. They must often react to dangerous situations very quickly.

When officers use dogs that have been trained in Europe, they must learn a foreign language! In Germany, for example, trainers speak German to their dogs. So the dogs learn commands that are in German. An American officer will need to use the same German words, because they were the words used in the dog's training.

▲ **When you become part of a K-9 team, you spend a lot of time with your dog—even if you're not fighting crime. This team lives in China, where there are more than 10,000 police dogs.**

《You could also become a veterinarian. You will have to go to school for many years. You can specialize in caring for large animals such as horses.》

Agency (FEMA) will help when disaster strikes. The agency may send in an Urban Search and Rescue (US&R) team to look for people trapped in buildings. These teams include search dogs and their handlers. Some handlers are civilians, and some work for local fire and police departments. All the handlers must get special training, just like the dogs.

Working with Animals

You don't have to become a police officer if you want to work with dogs, horses, or other animals. Some police departments, for example, have large mounted units. Since they

▲ **A police officer in Washington, D.C., trains a German shepherd to sniff out bombs. K-9 units have to keep training throughout their working lives.**

have a lot of horses, they hire grooms to work in their stables. A groom is someone who takes care of horses. You could also become a veterinarian. You will have to go to school for many years. You can specialize in caring for large animals such as horses. As a veterinarian, you will help make sure the animals stay healthy, giving them shots and testing them for diseases. You will also treat them if they get injured.

It is exciting to work in law enforcement or be on a search-and-rescue mission. But if you love animals, you can find many other ways to be part of an animal's life and to help people at the same time.

▲ **Police work can be dangerous, for both people and animals. Here, an officer helps an injured police dog after a bomb exploded in Northern Ireland.**

Glossary

aggressive
always ready to attack or fight

agile
able to move smoothly, easily, and quickly

alfalfa
a plant in the legume family (which includes peas and soybeans) that is widely grown for hay

batons
short, thick clubs that police officers carry for protection

domesticated
trained to live with or be used by human beings; tamed

draft horses
large, powerful horses that can pull heavy loads

foals
horses that are less than one year old

intimidating
causing fear

K-9 unit
a police officer and police dog who work together to fight crime

mounted police
officers who fight crime on horseback

paramedics
people who are trained to give medical treatment during an emergency

quarter horse
a horse named for its ability to beat any other type of horse in a quarter-mile race

track
to follow the scent of a particular person

veterinarian
a person who gives medical treatment to animals

yearlings
horses that are one year old

Further Information

BOOKS

Apte, Sunita. *Police Horses (Horse Power)*. New York: Bearport Publishing, 2007.

Barnes, Julia. *Horses at Work (Animals at Work)*. Milwaukee, WI: Gareth Stevens Publishing, 2005.

Criscione, Rachel Damon. *The Quarter Horse (The Library of Horses)*. New York: Powerkids Press, 2006.

Miller, Marie-Therese. *Police Dogs (Dog Tales: True Stories about Amazing Dogs)*. New York: Chelsea Clubhouse, 2007.

Ruffin, Francis E. *Police Dogs (Dog Heroes)*. New York: Bearport Publishing, 2005.

Murray, Julie. *Search-and-Rescue Animals (Going to Work: Animal Edition)*. Edina, MN: ABDO Publishing, 2009.

WEBSITES

http://people.howstuffworks.com/police-dog.htm/printable
This site has a lot of useful information about police dogs, such as the different breeds used, how the dogs are trained, and what a typical day is like for a K-9 unit.

www.jcsda.com/kids/index.html
Visit this site to learn about search-and-rescue (SAR) dogs and see many photos of them in action.

http://www.gmp.police.uk/mainsite/pages/mountedunit1.htm
At this site, you can learn about how the mounted police do their jobs in Greater Manchester, United Kingdom.

http://northernhorse.com/mcclelland/PatrolHorse.htm
This ranch in Canada trains horses for police work. Visit the ranch's site for photos and more information about training.

http://www.troopers.state.ny.us/Specialized_Services/Canine_Unit/
The New York State Police use many police dogs. At this site, click on "Canine Gallery" to see photos of them.

http://www.rcmp-grc.gc.ca/mr-ce
Royal Canadian Mounted Police: RCMP Musical Ride. Visit this site for more information about the Musical Ride and to see photos of a performance.

Index

PICTURE CREDITS
The photographs in this book are used by permission and through the courtesy of:

Alamy: 22 (Pat Canova), 29 (67photo), 55 (Peter Casolino)

Corbis: 6 (Louie Psihoyos/Science Faction), 7 (Dale Spartas), 11 (Photo Collection Alexander Alland Sr.), 13 (Tom Nebbia), 14 (Henny Ray Abrams/Reuters), 16 (Luo Li/Redlink), 19 (Dale Spartas), 20 (Bettmann), 25 (Jim Craigmyle), 28 (Karen Kasmauski/Science Faction), 36 (Stefan Wermuth/Reuters), 39 (Zou Zheng/XinHua Press), 45 (Paul A. Souders), 49 (Ralf-Finn Hestoft), 51 (Yves Forestier), 58 (Tom Nebbia), 59 (Paul McErlane/Reuters)

Dreamstime: 17 (Kiankhoon), 27 (Chris Johnson), 31 (Jose Gil), 38 (Mikhail Olykainen), 41 (Haak78), 42 (Djk), 43 (Alan Crosthwaite), 54 (Peter Kim)

FLPA: 8 (ImageBroker)

Fotolia: 15 (Cynoclub), 21(Jeff), 35 (Elite Photography), 52 (Aleksey Trefilov), 56 (Sergejs Nescsereckis)

Getty Images: 9 (Don Murray), 10 (Time & Life Pictures), 32 (Stephen Dunn), 33 (Philip Nealey), 37 (Norbert Millauer/AFP), 57 (China Photos)

iStockphoto: 2 (Jonathan Parry), 47 (Luis Santana)

Photoshot: 30 (UPPA), 48 (Xinhua)

Press Association: 44 (Matthew Fearn)

Rex Features: 23 (Peter MacDiarmid), 26, 46 (Steve Wood), 53 (EO/SAE/Keystone USA)

Stock.Xchang: 12 (Tony Rooney)

ABOUT THE AUTHOR
Jim Mezzanotte has written more than thirty books for children. He lives in Milwaukee, Wisconsin, where he loves playing with the family dog, Hallie.